Real People

George Washington

By Philip Abraham

Children's Press®
A Division of Scholastic Inc.
New York / Toronto / London / Auckland / Sydney
Mexico City / New Delhi / Hong Kong
Danbury, Connecticut

Photo Credits: Cover © Museum of the City of New York/Corbis; p. 5 Francis G. Mayer/Corbis; p. 7 © Bob Rowan, Progressive Image/Corbis; pp. 9, 11, 13, 15, 19 © Bettmann/Corbis; p. 17 © Corbis; p. 21 © Christie's Images/Corbis
Contributing Editor: Jennifer Silate
Book Design: Christopher Logan

Visit Children's Press on the Internet at:
http://publishing.grolier.com

Library of Congress Cataloging-in-Publication Data

Abraham, Philip, 1970–
George Washington / by Philip Abraham.
    p. cm. -- (Real people)
    Includes bibliographical references and index.
Summary: An easy-to-read biography of the first president of the United States.
    ISBN 0-516-23949-X (lib. bdg.) -- ISBN 0-516-23603-2 (pbk.)
    1. Washington, George, 1732–1799--Juvenile literature. 2. Presidents--United States--Biography--Juvenile literature. [1. Washington, George, 1732–1799. 2. Presidents.] I. Title II. Real people (Children's Press)

  E312.66 .A27 2002
  973.4'1'092--dc21
  [B]   2001032338

Contents

1 Mount Vernon   6

2 Martha Custis   8

3 President of the
United States   18

4 New Words   22

5 To Find Out More   23

6 Index   24

7 About the Author   24

This is George Washington.

He was the first **president** of the United States.

George Washington was born in 1732.

He lived in this house.

It is called Mount Vernon.

George married Martha
Custis in 1759.

They loved each other
very much.

George was a **soldier**.

He fought in many **battles**.

A **war** started **between** America and England.

George was the **leader** of the American **army**.

13

George was a very good leader.

America won the war.

15

Many people liked
George Washington.

George became the first president of the United States in 1789.

Today, we can see George's face on a dollar bill.

We will never forget George Washington.

21

New Words

army (**ar**-mee) a group of people
  trained to fight in a war
battles (**bat**-lz) fights between armies
between (bih-**tween**) having to do with
leader (**lee**-duhr) the person who is
  in charge
president (**prehz**-uh-duhnt) the person
  chosen to lead a country
soldier (**sohl**-juhr) a person in an army
war (**wor**) a fight between states
  or countries

22

To Find Out More

Books

George Washington: Soldier, Hero, President
by Justine and Ron Fontes
Dorling Kindersley Publishing

George Washington: A Picture Book Biography
by James Cross Giblin
Scholastic Trade

Web Sites

Mount Vernon
http://www.mountvernon.org/
This site has a tour of George Washington's home, Mount Vernon.

The American Presidency: George Washington
http://gi.grolier.com/presidents/aae/bios/01pwash.html
Learn many fun facts about the first president of the United States on this Web site.

23

Index

America, 12, 14
army, 12

battles, 10

Custis, Martha, 8

England, 12

leader, 12, 14

Mount Vernon, 6

president, 4, 18

soldier, 10

United States, 4, 18

war, 12, 14

About the Author

Philip Abraham is a freelance writer. He works in New York City.

Reading Consultants

Kris Flynn, Coordinator, Small School District Literacy, The San Diego County Office of Education

Shelly Forys, Certified Reading Recovery Specialist, W.J. Zahnow Elementary School, Waterloo, IL

Sue McAdams, Former President of the North Texas Reading Council of the IRA, and Early Literary Consultant, Dallas, TX